TABLE OF CONTENTS

On the Job at Sea

The *Time Bandit* pulls out of an Alaskan harbor in mid-February. It is headed to the Bering Sea for several weeks of fishing for crabs, or crabbing. This **commercial** fishing vessel is built to survive big 40-foot (12-meter) waves. It weighs 298 tons and is 113 feet (34.4 m) long. It's a good thing, because the ship will meet some of these waves during its trip.

The **galley** freezer and pantry are loaded with meat, cereal, and canned goods. **Deckhands** eat huge meals when they are out at sea. They work 18- to 20-hour shifts. The meals help them keep up their strength.

[21ST CENTURY SKILLS LIBRARY]

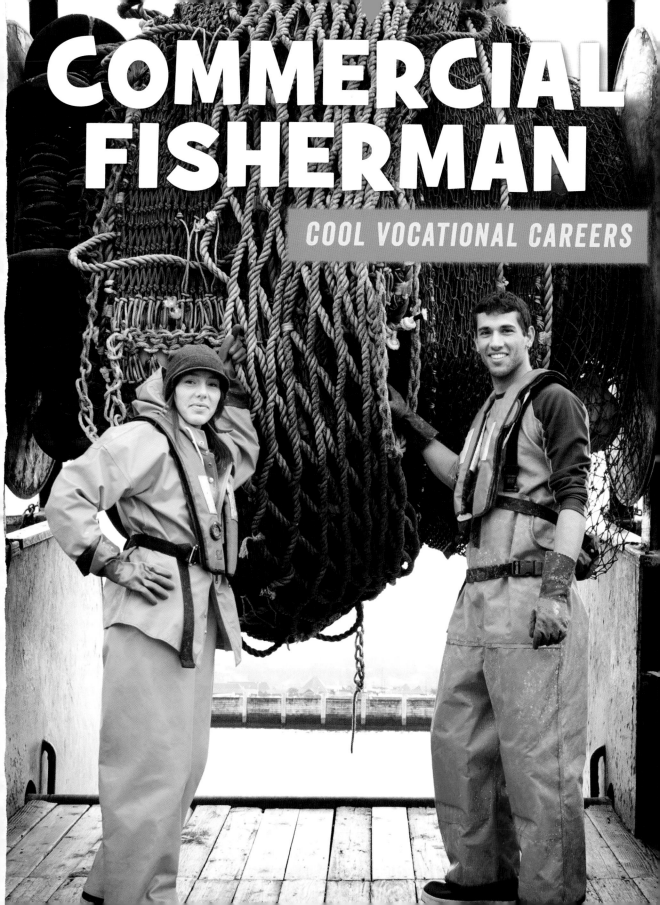

COMMERCIAL FISHERMAN

COOL VOCATIONAL CAREERS

Published in the United States of America by Cherry Lake Publishing
Ann Arbor, Michigan
www.cherrylakepublishing.com

Content Adviser: Kenny Walker, commercial fisherman in Valdez, Alaska
Reading Adviser: Marla Conn MS, Ed., Literacy specialist, Read-Ability, Inc.

Photo Credits: © CI2 / Alamy Stock Photo, cover, 1, 22; © Twildlife | Dreamstime.com, 5; © Vintagepix/Shutterstock, 6; © Signature Message/Shutterstock, 8; © spwidoff/Shutterstock, 11; © Andrea G. Karelias/Shutterstock, 12; © Anadolu Agency / Contributor / Getty Images, 14; © Design Pics Inc / Alamy Stock Photo, 17; © Predrag Vuckovic/istock, 18; © TTshutter/Shutterstock, 20; © David Hughes/Shutterstock, 25; © LFink/Shutterstock, 26; © Scott Dickerson/Newscom, 28

Library of Congress Cataloging-in-Publication Data
Names: Labrecque, Ellen.
Title: Commercial fisherman / Ellen Labrecque.
Description: Ann Arbor : Cherry Lake Publishing, 2016. |
Series: Cool vocational careers | Audience: Grades 4 to 6. | Includes bibliographical
    references and index.
Identifiers: LCCN 2015049650| ISBN 9781634710619 (hardcover) |
    ISBN 9781634711609 (paperback) | ISBN 9781634713580 (ebook)
Subjects: LCSH: Fishers—Juvenile literature. | Fisheries—Juvenile literature.
Classification: LCC HD8039.F65 L33 2016 | DDC 639.2023—dc23
LC record available at http://lccn.loc.gov/2015049650

Cherry Lake Publishing would like to acknowledge the work of the Partnership for 21st Century Learning.
Please visit *www.p21.org* for more information.

Printed in the United States of America
Corporate Graphics

ABOUT THE AUTHOR

Ellen Labrecque is a freelance writer living in Yardley, Pennsylvania. Previously, she was a senior editor at *Sports Illustrated Kids*. Ellen loves to travel and then learn about new places and people she can write about in her books.

Even a simple task on a boat can be life-threatening, so fishermen need common sense.

Crabs are caught in special cages called "pots," which come in all shapes and sizes.

The *Time Bandit* heads out far to the sea. Deckhands bait the bulky crab pots that will capture the crabs. The pots are 700-pound (317.5 kilograms) steel traps. They bait it with the types of fish that crabs like to eat, such as sardines, herring, and cod. Then they throw the pots into the water. A **buoy** marks the location of each crab pot. After the last pot is dropped, the ship returns to where the first pots were dropped and hauls them back up. A whole day may pass before a pot is brought back on deck. Hopefully, the pot will be full of crabs. Fishermen and women measure and sort the crabs. Crabs that are too small are released back into the sea.

Off the coast of California, Mike Hudson heads out to sea. He is in a 37.4-foot (11.4 m) vessel called the *Cash Flow II*. He and his wife, Yvette, fish for wild king salmon. They will fish about 75 miles (121 kilometers) offshore, but their job won't be easy. California has been facing **drought** conditions for the past couple of years. Salmon hatch in fresh river waters and migrate to the ocean. But there is less and less water to flush the salmon out to the sea. In years past, millions of salmon swam in the ocean off of California. In 2015, that number was estimated to be just 630,000.

21st Century Content

In 2012, U.S. commercial fishermen landed 9.6 billion pounds (4.4 billion kg) of seafood valued at $5.1 billion! Below are the top five states that caught the most.

- *Alaska (5.3 billion pounds) (2.4 billion kg)*
- *Louisiana (1.2 billion pounds) (544 million kg)*
- *Virginia (461.9 million pounds) (209.5 million kg)*
- *Washington (420.1 million pounds) (190.5 million kg)*
- *California (358.2 million pounds) (162.5 million kg)*

Oil can poison an area's animal population.

Peter Vujnovich heads into the Gulf of Mexico on his boat. He is one of more than 16,000 people in Louisiana who work in the fishing industry. In 2010, a massive oil spill occurred in the Gulf of Mexico. An oil spill can kill fish and other animals that live in and around water. Sea animals that do not die may still have poison from the oil in their bodies. Peter lost 70 percent of his oyster beds. The oil company responsible for the oil spill hired commercial fishing vessels to help control the oil. But it still took Peter 3 years to recover from his losses.

After most of the oil was cleaned from the water's surface and beaches, government agencies tested the fish and shellfish in the gulf to make sure it was safe to eat. Then Vujnovich and the rest of Louisiana's commercial fishermen and women went back to doing what they love.

What It Takes

Commercial fishing is often a family business. Many of today's fishermen and women learned their trade from their parents.

That was the case for James Blanchard, whose father taught him how to shrimp when he was just 12 years old. "I knew this is what I wanted to do when I got big," James said.

Most (if not all) people who have never worked at sea before start as greenhorns. But that is rare. Being a greenhorn on a boat can be a rough way to start. Greenhorns work long hours and are in charge of the **grunt work** on the boat, such as keeping it clean and preparing bait for the traps. Their tasks often depend on what time of year they are working, since many fishing vessels have different crews for each season. Someone who would like to start a career as a fisherman would want to find a vessel before or

Many fishermen grow up fishing with their parents and grandparents.

during salmon season. If the person works hard and shows great work **ethic**, the captain will offer the new greenhorn the same job but for another fishing season like crab or halibut. He or she will get better pay for the next season.

There are no education requirements for being a commercial fisher, but there are ways to improve your chances of getting hired. It is helpful to take courses in **navigation**, boat handling, and boat safety. Knowing how to repair machinery and radios is also a plus. First-aid skills are useful when accidents happen. Fishermen and women can learn these skills by taking classes at

The U.S. Coast Guard sets many rules about how many fish of each kind can be caught.

vocational schools and community colleges. Many fishermen today have not completed much formal education.

It might seem like being captain would be the best job on a commercial fishing vessel, but it is not an easy one. The captain works hard and is responsible for both the **catch** and the crew. Some captains own their vessels. Others are hired by owners to run ships. It is the captain's job to plan and oversee the fishing operation. This means finding the best fishing spots, making sure equipment is in good shape, managing the catch, and selling the fish.

21st Century Content

Overfishing is a big threat to the ocean's ecosystems. When ships overfish, they take too many fish from the ocean. There are fewer fish left to reproduce, which means different species of fish become endangered or even extinct. In Alaska, for example, there are several canneries and fishing vessels that don't always adhere to the laws and regulations. They're able to get away with it because of how huge the state is, and how remote they are. Laws have been established in the United States to make sure overfishing doesn't happen in the future.

A captain needs to be confident about using the navigation equipment.

Captains must be able to use a compass, read charts, and use electronic navigation equipment such as GPS systems. They also need to know how to use **sonar**. Sonar can track schools of fish and help the captain avoid underwater obstacles such as sandbars and reefs.

Fishermen are **conservationists** by nature. They understand the need to preserve their resources in order to preserve their way of life. Many commercial fishermen work with politicians, as well as environmental groups, to protect food and nonfood species and their habitat.

"I really like the overlap of the environmental ethic with the blue-collar worker," says Tim Sloane, executive director of the Pacific Coast Federation of Fishermen's Associations. "These fishermen, whose jobs are on the line, are the ones who want to clean up their ocean environment the most."

Dangerous Duties

Commercial fishing is demanding work. Hauling in fish or shellfish requires a strong, healthy body. When fishermen are out at sea for 2 months straight, they fish at all hours of the day and night. Sometimes they go to work after just 4 hours of sleep.

Some fishermen use **trawling** to catch fish. This is a dragging method that captures fish that live at the bottom of the ocean. Other fishermen use a purse **seine** to catch the fish. This kind of net forms into a pouch, trapping fish inside. Netting fish is hard work. It takes about 2 hours to set up the net and haul it back in. Crews work all night to put the net out four or five times.

Some fishermen **troll**, or use poles and lines to catch the fish. When Mike Hudson is out at sea, he has as many as 40 lines in the water at one time.

Emptying nets is a tough part of the job.

Nets sometimes catch animals they aren't supposed to.

Unfortunately, sometimes the nets and lines catch unwanted marine life such as dolphins and turtles, and even small sharks, starfish, and jellyfish. This is called **bycatch**, and it happens pretty often. But more and more technology is being invented that is stopping this from occurring. Also, most fishermen now use barbless hooks. If they do catch an unwanted fish or marine animal, they can release it back into the water unharmed.

Many things can go wrong on a fishing trip. Bad weather limits the amount of fish caught. Nets tear, machines break, and people get hurt. Sonar can help find fish, but it only works if the fish are nearby. These can all reduce a fishing trip's success.

Commercial fishing is one of the most dangerous jobs in the world. Bad storms and high seas can sink boats. Many boats are on automatic pilot as they fish. This can lead to collisions with other boats. High winds and waves can knock a fisherman right off the deck. Drowning is always a big fear! The Coast Guard tries to keep fishing vessels safe, but there is no guarantee.

Twenty-four commercial fishermen were killed on the job in 2014. This gave commercial fishing the second-highest death rate of all jobs in the United States. (Loggers had the highest death rate). Most serious fishing accidents happen when crews are

Life and Career Skills

The Monterey Bay Aquarium in California has created a Web site called Seafood Watch. It recommends seafood to eat that has been caught or raised in ways that have had the least impact on the environment. If the seafood is labeled green, this is the best choice. If it is labeled yellow, it is okay to buy, although not the best choice. If the seafood is labeled red, you should not buy it because it has been overfished. Check out different fish at seafoodwatch.org!

In a storm, a little boat could be in big danger.

spreading or pulling in fishing gear. Deckhands have gotten caught in nets and suffered broken bones or deep cuts. Injuries are also common in canneries.

An experienced commercial fisherman or woman may earn about $44,000 per year. The average salary is about $37,000 a year. Most deckhands are paid by the day or by a percentage of the profit. Getting pay by the percentage of the profit is what most fishermen prefer, though there is more risk. It offers more rewarding pay if the crew can bring in large catches. Pay is based on the worker's experience and the length and difficulty of the job. Trips can last anywhere from a few days to several months. A day fee might be as much as $700 for some jobs.

Pay for commercial fishing work sometimes depends on two factors. The first is how much it costs to run the vessel. The second is how many fish the vessel catches. One crew might spend a week at sea and catch as many fish as they are legally allowed to take. Another crew could spend the same amount of time and catch very little.

The cost of running a fishing vessel can affect how much money commercial fishermen earn. Fishing vessels are expensive in Alaska, where fishing is a big business. Then there is the cost of

Commercial fishermen can make a lot of money in a short period of time.

the nets, fuel, food, and safety equipment. Captains may also need permits to fish in certain areas. These permits can cost thousands of dollars.

Nature's Rules

Commercial fishing was once a huge opportunity. There were few rules or laws. Fishermen got rich whaling, catching salmon, or pulling in tuna. That is no longer the case. It is much harder to make a profit in today's commercial fishing industry. However, the appeal is that the business allows people to make a lot of money in a very short amount of time. The fishermen also visit beautiful remote locations, make friends from all over the world, and build excellent work ethics.

The law requires fishing vessels and their captains to have licenses or permits. Each state sets its own rules for licenses. These rules can get complicated. Louisiana created an educational program for fishermen and women in their state to help them stay updated on the laws. The program, called Louisiana Fisheries

Valdez, Alaska, is a popular spot for commercial fishing vessels.

Forward, helps fishermen understand the latest regulations and even the latest in fishing equipment and technology.

Other states' laws are different than Louisiana's. Most states only give out a certain number of licenses. New fishers cannot just buy a new license and go fishing. They must buy an existing license from someone who is willing to sell his or hers. Because most fishermen and women love being at sea, there are few licenses for sale.

Fishing seasons and species **quotas** are newer ideas. In the past, fishing crews would catch as many fish or shellfish as their

The Coast Guard helps keep fishermen safe at sea.

vessels could hold. No one thought that the oceans might run out of them. However, certain areas and species were overfished, which has an impact on which kinds of fish are caught these days. Today, states set quotas on different fish species. A quota may limit the amount of fish a crew can catch in a certain time period. It might also place a limit on what size the fish can be. For example, a crew might only be allowed to keep fish that are more than 18 inches (45.7 centimeters) long.

Experts keep track of how many fish are caught. The quotas are adjusted to make sure that all fish species will continue to survive. Chilean sea bass, Atlantic salmon, swordfish, and dozens of other species have all had quotas. "The regulations are actually fantastic," says Mike Hudson. "They just make sure we don't take more fish than we should. After all, if we have no more fish to catch, our jobs are worthless."

The commercial fishing industry has put people in charge of making sure there will be enough fish for people to eat in the future. Many environmental organizations work to make sure this happens, too. One place where conservation activists successfully fixed a potential problem is Bristol Bay, Alaska.

Life and Career Skills

The U.S. Coast Guard knows how dangerous commercial fishing can be. It works to keep fishermen and women safe by offering free training to prepare fishermen for dangerous situations at sea. The two-day training is offered all over the country and teaches things such as how to retrieve a fisherman who has fallen into the water and how to shoot off smoke signals in times of distress. The goal of these classes is simple: Bring all fishermen home safely.

If the fishermen aren't careful, overfishing can lead to severe environmental problems.

Politicians had proposed to build an open-pit mine near rivers that flow directly into Bristol Bay. The mine, which would gain access to copper and gold deposits, could have polluted the bay, home to the world's most productive salmon.

"It's probably the largest and most pristine of all the salmon fisheries in the world," Ray Hilborn, a fisheries professor at the University of Washington, said about the bay. "You couldn't design a system better for salmon."

Thanks to the work of the Environmental Protection Agency and an organization called Trout Unlimited, the building of this

[21ST CENTURY SKILLS LIBRARY]

mine was put on hold. Alaska's fishermen hope this hold lasts forever. "All the mine is going to do is kill our fisheries," said one fisherman. "There's no way to do it safely."

Increased costs and decreased amounts of fish make it harder for commercial fishermen and women to profit. New rules, conservation issues, and higher fuel prices can also make things difficult. However, the worldwide demand for seafood continues to rise. Trout Unlimited follows this motto: "Take care of the fish, then the fishing will take care of itself." All commercial fishermen and women believe in this slogan, too! Because for them, fishing isn't a career—it's a way of life.

Think About It

Fishing is one of the oldest jobs humans have ever had. Fish was also some of the earliest foods for humans. Why do you think this is the case? Were there food stores to shop in long ago?

Learn more online about ocean animals. Which ones are your favorites? Why do you think it is so important to do your part to preserve our oceans? Make a list of ways you can help protect natural resources.

Have you ever eaten fish before? What kind was it? If you haven't, think about what kind of fish you might like to try someday. Look online to learn more about this kind of fish—where it lives, how it's caught, and how it's cooked.

For More Information

BOOKS

DK Publishing. *Ocean: A Visual Encyclopedia*. New York: DK Publishing, 2015.

Howard, Melanie. *Freshwater Fishing for Kids*. North Mankato, MN: Capstone Press, 2013.

WEB SITES

Ocean Conservancy
www.oceanconservancy.org
Discover ways that you can help preserve our oceans and seas and the species that live there.

Save Our Seas Foundation
www.saveourseas.com
Learn more about marine research, conservation, and education.

Voices from the Fisheries
www.st.nmfs.noaa.gov/voicesfromthefisheries
Hear what fishermen and women have to say about their work and their lives.

GLOSSARY

buoy (BOO-ee) a large plastic floating marker

bycatch (BYE-kach) unwanted animals that are trapped when fishing

catch (KACH) the total number of fish caught on a fishing trip

commercial (kuh-MUR-shuhl) having to do with business

conservationists (kon-ser-VAY-shuh-nists) people who work to protect natural resources such as rivers, forests, and oceans

deckhands (DEK-handz) sailors who perform work that requires intelligence, strength, and a lot of energy

drought (DROUT) a long period without rain

ethic (ETH-ik) a belief that something is very important

galley (GAL-ee) a kitchen on a ship, plane, or camper

grunt work (GRUHNT WORK) tasks that are tough, dirty, and repetitive

navigation (na-vuh-GAY-shuhn) the art of plotting the route of a ship or aircraft

quotas (KWOH-tuhs) limits on amounts of something

seine (SAYN) a type of fishing net that closes up like a pouch

sonar (SOH-nahr) a method for detecting objects and fish in water using sound waves

trawling (TRAW-ling) fishing with a net along the seafloor

troll (TROHL) to fish with a rod and line

vocational (voh-KAY-shuh-nuhl) relating to special skills and training for a particular job

INDEX